Published in the United States of America by The Child's World®
PO Box 326 • Chanhassen, MN 55317-0326
800-599-READ • www.childsworld.com

My First Steps to Math™ is a registered trademark of Scholastic, Inc.
Page 22 artwork by Ellen Sasaki

Library of Congress Cataloging-in-Publication Data
Moncure, Jane Belk.
My ten book / by Jane Belk Moncure.
p. cm. — (My first steps to math)
ISBN 1-59296-665-9 (lib. bdg. : alk. paper)
1. Counting—Juvenile literature. 2. Number concept—Juvenile literature. I. Title.
QA113.M668 2006
513.2'11—dc22
2005025700

My ten Book

by Jane Belk Moncure
illustrated by John Jones

This is Little ten .

Little  lives in the house of ten.

It has ten rooms. Count them.

Little  likes to take walks.

One day, she walks to her mailbox.
She finds a letter.

It says:

January 10

Dear Friend,
I have sent
you ten
surprises!
Love,
A secret pal

Soon a delivery van
comes down the road.
Guess what is inside?

Little  gets a big box. The tag reads, "Have fun, Little Ten!"

Little  takes the box indoors. Inside the box are ten robot dolls.

"What a super gift!" she says.

Little  has five girl dolls
and five boy dolls.

Count them.

"I love my new dolls! I will play with them
all year long," says Little Ten.

Little  has a tea party
for her dolls.

There is a muffin for each doll.
How many muffins are there?

One snowy day, Little 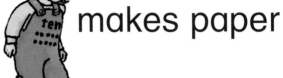 makes paper hats for her dolls.

She paints five hats blue.

How many hats does she paint pink?

Little  has a doll parade.

"How nice my dolls look,"
she says.

Count her dolls as they march two by two.

One sunny and wintry day, Little takes her dolls . . .

for a ride on her sled.

"Look at the clean white snow," she says.

Oops! Four dolls fall off the sled.

How many stay on
the sled? Count them.

Little  puts the four dolls back on the sled.

On the first day of spring, Little takes her dolls . . .

for a ride in her wagon.

"Look at all the birds and the pretty flowers," she says.

Little  wants to pick a flower for each doll.

She picks seven flowers.
How many more does she need?

On the first day of summer, Little takes her dolls to the seashore.

She builds a big sand castle.

It has lots of towers. Count them.

Little  wants to collect a shell for each doll.

She finds six shells.

How many more does she need?

On the last day of summer, Little  makes a picnic lunch
for her dolls.

She makes five big sandwiches.

She cuts them in half.

How many half sandwiches does she have for her dolls? Count them.

Little 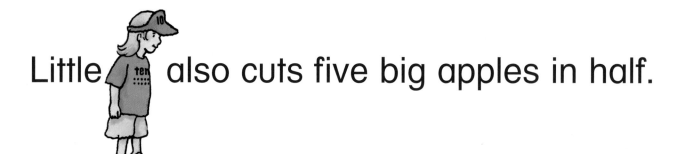 also cuts five big apples in half.

Does each doll have half of a sandwich and half of an apple?

Count them.

On the first day of autumn, Little takes her dolls for a walk.

"It is cooler outside. The leaves are starting to fall," she said.

Little  wants to collect a pretty leaf for each doll.

She finds eight leaves.

How many more does she need?

On the first day of winter, Little
decides to give her dolls
a big present.

The dolls
open the
present.

Guess what is inside?

It is a house for the dolls.

"What a super surprise!"
they say.

How many rooms does the house have?

Little  found ten of everything.

ten dolls

ten paper hats

ten towers

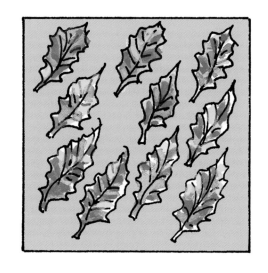

ten leaves

Now you find ten things.

Let's add with Little  ten.

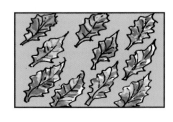 +  =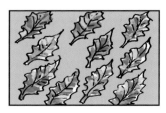

10 + 0 = 10

 +  =

5 + 5 = 10

Now take away.

10   –   1   =   9

10   –   0   =   10

Little 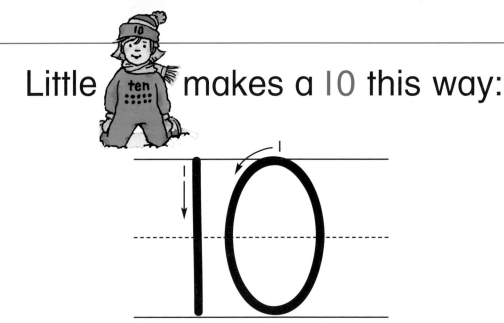 makes a 10 this way:

She makes the number word like this:

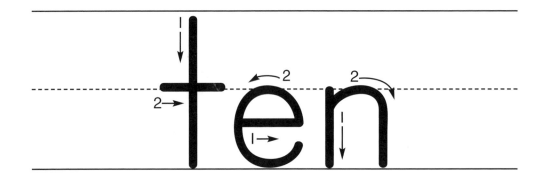

You can make them in the air with your finger.